D0578858

Badgers

and Other Mustelids

Book Author: Lisa Klobuchar

For World Book:

Editorial: Paul A. Kobasa, Maureen Liebenson, Christine Sullivan
Research: Andy Roberts, Loranne Shields
Graphics and Design: Melanie Bender, Sandra Dyrlund
Photos: Tom Evans, Sylvia Ohlrich
Permissions: Janet Peterson
Indexing: David Pofelski
Proofreading: Anne Dillon
Pre-press and Manufacturing: Carma Fazio, Anne Fritzinger, Steve Hueppchen, Madelyn Underwood

**For information about other World Book publications, visit our Web site at
http://www.worldbook.com, or call 1-800-WORLDBK (967-5325).**

**For information about sales to schools and libraries, call 1-800-975-3250 (United States);
1-800-837-5365 (Canada).**

World Book, Inc.
233 N. Michigan Avenue
Chicago, IL 60601
U.S.A.

Library of Congress Cataloging-in-Publication Data

Badgers and other mustelids.
     p. cm. -- (World Book's animals of the world)
   Includes bibliographical references and index.
   ISBN 0-7166-1265-8 -- ISBN 0-7166-1261-5
    1. Badgers--Juvenile literature. 2. Mustelidae--Juvenile literature.
  I. Title. II. World Book, Inc. II. Series.

   QL737 .C25B249 2005
   599.76'7--dc22

                               2004015690

Printed in Malaysia
1 2 3 4 5 6 7 8 09 08 07 06 05

Picture Acknowledgments: Cover: © Tom Brakefield, Corbis; © D. Robert & Lorrie Franz, Corbis; © Thomas Kitchin, Tom Stack & Associates; © Gerard Lacz, Animals Animals; © Rich Reid, Animals Animals.

© Erwin & Peggy Bauer, Animals Animals 35; © Erwin & Peggy Bauer, Tom Stack & Associates 5, 53; © Peter Baumann, Animals Animals 27; © Tom Brakefield, Corbis 4, 31; © Hans Dieter Brandl, Frank Lane Picture Agency/Corbis 33; © Alan Carey, Photo Researchers 3, 17; © W. Perry Conway, Corbis 19, 21; © Michael Francis 29; © D. Robert & Lorrie Franz, Corbis 10; © John Giustina, Bruce Coleman Inc. 61; © Cathy & Gordon Illig, Animals Animals 51; © Kevin Keatley, Nature Picture Library 25; © Thomas Kitchin, Tom Stack & Associates 45, 55; © Gerard Lacz, Animals Animals 43; © Pat & Tom Leeson, Photo Researchers 39; © Zig Leszczynski, Animals Animals 57; © Joe McDonald, Tom Stack & Associates 15; © Tom Murphy, SuperStock 41; © Rich Reid, Animals Animals 37; © Juergen & Christine Sohn, Animals Animals 59; © Mark Stouffer, Animals Animals 49; © John Tinning, Frank Lane Picture Agency/Corbis 13; © Terry Whittaker, Photo Researchers 5, 47.

Illustrations: WORLD BOOK illustration by John Fleck 7. Illustration of a sett on page 23 by John Fleck, based upon research and diagrams provided by T. J. Roper, University of Sussex.

Badgers
and Other Mustelids

Can you guess why I am so good at digging?

World Book, Inc.
a Scott Fetzer company
Chicago

Contents

What do you mean? I don't smell anything!

I am one long, fine-looking animal.

Pooh and I have the same favorite food.

What Is a Mustelid?

A mustelid *(MUHS tuh lid)* is a type of mammal. Another name for the mustelid family is the weasel family. Members of this family include badgers, ermines *(UR muhnz)*, ferrets, fishers, grisons *(GRY suhnz)*, minks, otters, polecats, ratels *(RAY tuhls)*, sables, skunks, weasels, and wolverines.

Nearly all mustelids have glands near their rump that make a smelly liquid that is sometimes called musk. And most members of this family have a long, slim body and short legs. This body shape allows mustelids to follow their prey into small holes and narrow cracks.

Mustelids come in many sizes. The largest weasel relatives are sea otters, giant otters, and wolverines. Sea otters may weigh up to 85 pounds (39 kilograms); giant otters can reach 75 pounds (34 kilograms); and wolverines can grow up to 55 pounds (25 kilograms). By contrast, the smallest weasel relative is the least weasel—it weighs about 2 ounces (57 grams).

weasel

badger

otter

ferret

skunk

wolverine

Where in the World Do Badgers and Other Mustelids Live?

Badgers can be found in Asia, Europe, and North America.

American badgers live in southwestern Canada, in the United States from the West Coast to the Midwest, and south to central Mexico. They make their homes mostly in dry country or grasslands with few trees.

Old World badgers live throughout Europe and in northern Asia. Old World badgers prefer to live in forested areas.

Ferret badgers, hog badgers, and stink badgers live in the mountains and forests of southeastern Asia. And, although not a true badger, a similar mustelid that is known as the ratel, or honey badger, can be found in Africa.

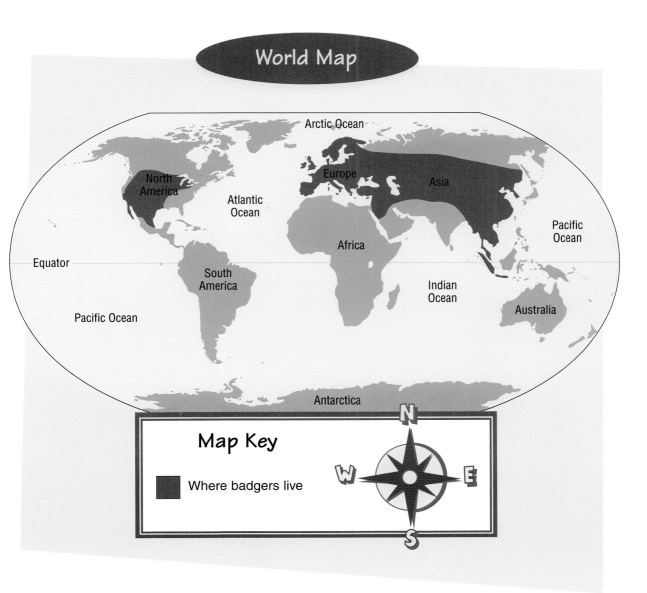

World Map

Arctic Ocean

North America

Europe

Asia

Atlantic Ocean

Pacific Ocean

Africa

Equator

South America

Indian Ocean

Pacific Ocean

Australia

Antarctica

Map Key

Where badgers live

N

W   E

S

How Can You Tell
It's a Badger?

A badger has a short, broad body and a short, bushy tail. It has long claws on its feet. Badgers generally have white and black markings on their head and face.

The American badger has gray or reddish fur and a white stripe running up from its nose. The Old World badger is usually gray on its back, but its underside and legs are black. It has a white face with two dark stripes that run up each side of its face, over its eyes.

American badger

What Is Special About a Badger's Body?

Most badgers have a strong, stout body with short legs. Their front legs are especially strong. Their front paws are equipped with long, sharp claws for digging. Badgers need these digging tools because they often dig for their meals. Badgers also live underground and dig large burrows and tunnels.

Badgers have small eyes and ears. Their hearing is good. Their sense of smell is excellent compared to their other senses, but their eyesight is weak.

All badgers have glands near their rumps that produce a strong-smelling liquid called musk. Some types of badgers squirt out musk to drive away attackers. Badgers also use musk to mark their territory or to mark a scent trail to a source of food or other important places. That way they can find their way around using mainly their noses.

A badger's front paw

 13

How Does a Badger Defend Itself?

Badgers, like most animals, will first try to get away when attacked. They cannot run fast, but they can dig their way to safety at a surprising speed.

They may also try to frighten an attacker by fluffing up their own fur, hissing or growling, and baring their teeth.

All badgers make smelly musk that may be released to defend against an attacker, but stink badgers can squirt their musk at an attacker. If an animal attacks one of these badgers and gets blasted with burning, stinking musk, that animal will think twice before it attacks a stink badger again.

If none of these actions drives off the attacker, badgers can fight back with their strong jaws and powerful teeth. They can give an attacker a nasty bite. Badgers also have tough, loose skin. Because the skin is so loose, the badger can twist around and bite the attacker, even if the attacker has the badger's skin in a tight hold by the teeth.

American badger

Are Badgers Meat-eaters?

Badgers are included in a group named carnivores *(KAHR nuh vawrz)*, which means "meat-eaters." But, badgers and many other animals in this group are actually omnivores *(OM nuh vawrz)*, or animals that eat both meat and plants.

One of the Old World badger's favorite meals is a fat, wriggly earthworm. Why? One reason is that earthworms come to the surface at night, when badgers are out hunting for food. An earthworm in the grass is easy for a badger to gobble up, much easier than digging for rodents. On a damp night, earthworms are plentiful, and a badger can eat its fill with very little effort. Earthworms are also a great source of nutrients.

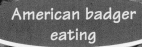

American badger
eating

In What Kind of Home Does a Badger Live?

All species of badgers live underground, in burrows. But not all badger burrows are alike. Ferret badgers, hog badgers, and stink badgers dig simple burrows. These burrows have one chamber that is large enough for a badger to sleep in or to allow for a mother badger to give birth and care for her young.

The burrows of American badgers may have a few side tunnels branching off the main tunnel. American badgers also may dig several separate burrows in different parts of their large territory. They move from one burrow to another.

Old World badgers, however, dig the most amazing burrows, called setts. Setts can spread over many acres, and may have over 80 entrances. Most setts, however, have about 10 entrances.

American badger looking out from burrow

How Does a Badger Dig?

Badgers carefully choose the place for their burrows. They like to dig their burrows on the side of a slope. This helps water drain away and keeps the burrow dry. The largest burrows are dug in places with soft soil where it is easy to dig. Often, badgers simply enlarge old burrows by digging new tunnels that connect with old ones. They'll also enlarge the abandoned burrows of other animals, such as rabbits.

The badger uses its strong claws to break up the earth. When it has broken up a small pile of dirt, the badger scoots backward out of the tunnel, pushing the soil with its back legs as it goes. Then it kicks this loose soil into a pile outside of the burrow. Badgers can even push, drag, or carry heavy rocks out of the tunnel.

American badger
digging a burrow

What Is It Like
Inside a Sett?

The setts of Old World badgers are like underground apartment complexes. These setts are made up of lots of connected tunnels. The tunnels provide a way for badgers to travel safely underground. Wider areas within the tunnels, called chambers, provide places where badgers can sleep, give birth, and raise their young. Badgers drag dried grass, moss, leaves, or ferns into the chambers to make cozy beds. Year after year, badgers add new chambers and tunnels to their setts. In Europe, some badger setts are more than 100 years old.

Badgers keep their setts clean. They relieve themselves in areas outside of the sett. And, every once in a while, the badgers drag their bedding out of the chambers and let it air out in the sun. In addition to their underground homes, Old World badgers occasionally create aboveground nests. These areas are often located near sources of food. They are full of nesting material and are used as temporary resting places.

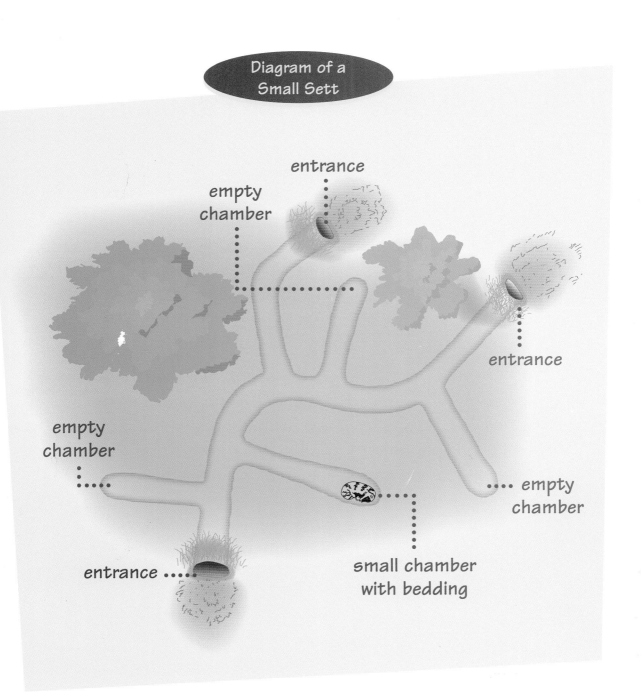

Diagram of a
Small Sett

entrance

empty
chamber

empty
chamber

entrance

empty
chamber

entrance

small chamber
with bedding

23

What Goes On in Old World Badger Families?

Old World badgers live together in a group called a clan. Clans are usually made up of about 10 animals, including adults and young. Each clan usually has a few adult males, or boars, a few adult females, or sows, and a few young, called cubs. When the young males are mature, they usually leave to join other clans. Young females usually stay with their birth clans.

Old World badgers use the scent from their musk glands to recognize each other. Each badger's musk smells a bit different. When all the badgers in a clan put their musk on one another, their scents get mixed together. As a result, each clan has its own unique scent. Each clan member bears the scent of the clan as well as its own scent. That is how Old World badgers recognize members of their own clan.

Old World badger family
foraging at night

How Do Baby Badgers Grow?

American and Old World badger cubs are born in the late winter or spring. They are usually born in litters of two or three. They are blind and covered with a thin coat of silvery fur. The mother badger nurses her babies—that is, she feeds them with milk from her body—for the first several weeks of their life. The cubs open their eyes after about a month.

As her cubs grow, an Old World badger mother starts to feed them by bringing up chewed food from her stomach for them to eat. An American badger mother, on the other hand, will bring back dead prey for her young to eat.

Soon, the cubs are ready to leave their home. At first they stay near the entrance. Then they start to explore farther from the burrow or sett, learning how to find food.

By the time Old World badgers are about 4 months old, they can take care of themselves. American badgers do not live in clans, and the young leave their mother after they are about 2 months old.

Three badger cubs

What Is the "Partnership" Between Coyotes and American Badgers?

Throughout Canada, the United States, and Mexico, people have observed an odd relationship between badgers and coyotes.

Both coyotes and badgers eat small burrowing animals, such as ground squirrels and prairie dogs. The coyote can chase the squirrels and catch them if they are running around aboveground. The badger, on the other hand, is not fast enough to catch a running ground squirrel. If the ground squirrel is hiding in its burrow, however, it may be safe from the coyote—but not from the badger. The badger can easily dig into a ground squirrel burrow.

A coyote sometimes will watch a badger as it digs for prey. While the badger digs, the prey may run out of its burrow as it tries to escape. Once out in the open, the prey becomes an easy meal for the coyote. Coyotes and badgers do not hunt together in the cooperative sense, but coyotes do benefit from the activities of badgers.

28

Badger with coyotes

 29

Why Are Mustelids So Smelly?

Most mustelids produce smelly musk. They use it mainly to mark their territory. Badgers, for example, mark their food-finding routes with musk so they can find their way around easily. Wolverines mark stashes of food with their musk so other animals will not want to eat it.

Mustelids also use musk for self-defense. The smell of skunks' and stink badgers' musk is really strong. These animals can spray their musk a distance of several feet. For example, when a striped skunk is being attacked, it gives plenty of warning before it sprays. It stamps its feet and raises its fur and tail. Then it bends its body so that its face and rump are both facing its enemy. If the enemy is not scared by this display, the striped skunk sprays a stream of musk. The bad smell can travel for more than a mile. If the musk gets into another animal's eyes, it causes burning pain. If breathed in, it can make a predator sick.

Striped skunk

How Do Mustelids Have Fun?

Many mustelids are playful, especially when they are young. Play is important to animals that hunt for their food. It helps them learn such skills as tracking and catching prey.

Otters and badgers get the prize for being the most playful members of the family. River otters wrestle and romp together. They splash around in the water and chase one another. Otters love to slide. In the summer, they slide down mudbanks on their bellies. In the winter, they slide down snowbanks and scurry through snow tunnels.

Badgers are very playful, too, especially the cubs. They seem to enjoy games of chase and play-fighting, with much nipping, growling, and tumbling around. They also have been seen playing the badger version of king-of-the-hill. In king-of-the-hill, one badger stands on a log or small mound of earth and another tries to knock it off. They also play with objects, such as cans and other human-made objects, that they may find.

European river otters at play

 33

What Are the Enemies of These Animals?

Badgers and their relatives hunt and feed on all sorts of small animals, including rattlesnakes. But some kinds of animals happily eat mustelids for dinner. So mustelids have to be on the lookout for bobcats, bears, wolves, foxes, cougars, and birds of prey, such as hawks and eagles.

Badger relatives that are active at night, such as skunks, weasels, and martens, are hunted by owls. Eagles and hawks kill ferrets, weasels, minks, and the babies of badgers and all their relatives.

White sharks sometimes attack and kill sea otters. But otters do not seem to be the sharks' favorite food. Scientists believe that white sharks bite otters and then let them go. Otters' lean, furry bodies do not have the filling fat that the sharks like to eat.

Badger confronting
a rattlesnake

Which Mustelid Floats Around on Its Back?

Sea otters live in the North Pacific Ocean, off the west coast of North America and the east coast of Siberia. These animals float around on their back, using their webbed back feet to paddle about in the sea. When napping, sea otters often wrap themselves in kelp (a kind of seaweed) to prevent drifting during their sleep. When hungry, they dive to the ocean floor to get their food. They can stay underwater for up to four minutes.

Sea otters spend almost their whole life at sea. They come ashore only rarely, to rest on rocks. They eat, sleep, and raise their young in the water.

Keeping warm is important for mammals that live in the ocean. Other mammals that live in the ocean, such as seals, whales, and dolphins, have a layer of fat, called blubber, under their skin. Blubber keeps these animals warm and helps them stay afloat. Otters do not have blubber, but their thick fur holds a lot of air. This layer of air acts like blubber to help otters stay afloat and keep warm.

36

Sea otter

Why Does a Sea Otter Carry a Rock?

Sea otters eat seafood. Their diet includes fish, octopuses, and squids. But they also eat a lot of shellfish, including abalones, clams, crabs, sea snails, and mussels. Sea otters grab shellfish with their front paws rather than with their mouths.

To open the hard shell of a shellfish, a sea otter places a rock on its own chest. The sea otter then uses its paws to pound the shellfish on the rock. When the shell breaks open, the sea otter can eat the soft body of the shellfish. A sea otter also uses its large, flat back teeth to crush hard shells.

Sea otter with a rock for shellfish

Which of These Animals Can Climb Trees?

Many mustelids are good climbers. Spotted skunks sometimes live in hollow trees. Wolverines are known to stash food in trees. Even badgers can climb trees.

But the best tree climbers in this group of animals are the pine martens. These mustelids live in the pine forests of northern Europe and North America. They leap and scamper high in the tree branches, where they capture their favorite prey animals— sleeping squirrels.

The fisher is another member of the weasel family that is quite at home in the treetops. Of the animals the fisher preys upon, there is one that few others will attempt to hunt—the porcupine. The body of a porcupine is covered with sharp spines, called quills, which can cause painful wounds to attackers. But fishers are quick enough to avoid the quills. A fisher usually attacks a porcupine on the ground. But if it needs to get a better angle on its prey, a fisher may climb up a tree and jump down on a porcupine.

Two pine martens
in a tree

How Do These Animals Spend the Winter?

Most mustelids are quite active all year around. In winter, ermines have been seen scurrying around in snow tunnels. Otters fish under the ice, sometimes swimming long distances before they come up for air through a break in the ice.

Wolverines have large, flat, wide paws that help them walk on top of snow. They are able to hunt large animals, such as deer and sheep, in the winter, because wolverines can move faster in the snow than can the larger animals. Wolverines store food for the winter by stashing it in trees or burying it under the snow or earth.

American badgers often spend most of the winter resting. In winter, food is harder to find. So in the summer and fall, badgers eat as much as they can. This helps their bodies store fat to get ready for winter. In winter, badgers may sleep in their burrows for days or weeks at a time. They can live off fat stored in their body. Skunks that live where the winters are very cold also spend most of the winter in their burrows.

Wolverine in snow

Which Mustelid Changes Color in the Winter?

Weasels that live in places with cold, snowy winters get a new "suit of clothes" every winter. These include the ermine (also called the short-tailed weasel), the least weasel, and the long-tailed weasel.

During the summer these weasels' fur is brown. But in winter, when the land is blanketed in white, the weasels turn white, too. Their white fur blends in with the snow and makes it hard for enemies to spot them.

How does the fur turn white? Certain substances produced in these weasels' skin cells give their fur its brown color. These substances are made only in the summer. As summer draws to a close, the skin stops making these chemicals. In the fall, as the brown fur is shed, it is replaced by new white fur.

An ermine in its winter phase

Whose Favorite Food Is Honey?

Ratels are members of the weasel family. Ratels live mainly in eastern and southern Africa. They are often called honey badgers because they resemble badgers and they love to eat honey.

Ratels can climb trees to reach beehives. Their sharp claws make it easy for them to break open a hive. Their tough skin protects them from bee stings. Then they can feast on the honey as well as the bees.

A ratel often finds a beehive with help from a bird called the honey guide. Honey guides eat the honey, bees, and beeswax found in beehives, but they can have trouble getting inside the hive. So, if a honey guide sees a ratel in the area, it gives out a special call that leads the ratel to the hive. When the ratel arrives, it tears open the hive and the two animals feed. Besides honey, ratels also eat small animals, including mammals, birds, reptiles, and insects, as well as some types of plants.

Ratel

Which Weasel Relative Is the Strongest?

Many stories are told about the wolverine's strength, intelligence, and fearlessness. Trappers tell stories of wolverines that figured out how to spring traps and steal the animals caught in them. Wolverines have also been accused of breaking into cabins and stealing food. Many of these stories, however, are probably exaggerated.

It is no exaggeration that the wolverine is the strongest animal of its size. It has a heavy body with powerful limbs. According to some estimates, if a wolverine were the size of a bear, it would be the strongest creature on Earth. The wolverine is a good climber and swimmer, but it spends most of its time on the ground.

Wolverines used to be widespread. But today these animals are quite rare. The southern boundary of their range has been pushed far to the north, and today they live only in far northern North America, north Asia, northern Europe, and in some parts of the western United States.

Wolverine

Why Is the Wolverine Also Called the Glutton?

Glutton is a word for a person who eats too much. Another common name for the wolverine is the glutton, because this animal can eat a lot of food at one time. Wolverines often live in far northern areas. In winter, food can be hard to find. So when food is available, a wolverine gobbles down as much as it can. Wolverines can kill large animals, such as reindeer, moose, or wild sheep. But they mostly eat carrion, small animals, birds and eggs, and berries.

Wolverines have strong jaws and sharp teeth. They can easily crush bones and chew frozen meat. People have reported that wolverines can bite through tin cans. They are strong enough to drag a load of meat three times their own weight.

Wolverines can steal prey from much larger animals, such as mountain lions, wolves, and bears. They scare off these animals by raising their tails, fluffing up their fur, and growling.

Wolverine feeding

Which Ferret Is a Mustelid?

The black-footed ferret is the only wild mustelid that is called a ferret. In the past, black-footed ferrets were common on the Great Plains of North America. Today, they are endangered. The main reason they have disappeared is that their lives depend almost completely on prairie dogs.

Prairie dogs are medium-sized rodents that live in large networks of burrows called prairie dog towns, or colonies. Nearly all of the black-footed ferret's diet is made up of prairie dogs. Ferrets hunt by night. They slip into prairie dog burrows and kill their prey when they are asleep.

Since the 1800's, people have destroyed most prairie dog towns. They did this because farmers and ranchers see prairie dogs as pests. Prairie dogs can eat a lot of the vegetation (plants) that grow on a piece of land. And, if a livestock animal steps into a prairie dog hole, it can break its leg. When the prairie dogs began to disappear, however, so did the black-footed ferrets.

Black-footed ferret

Which Member of This Family Is Extinct?

As with many animal families, some mustelids that lived long ago have become extinct. Most extinctions occurred naturally. Not too long ago, however, humans were responsible for the extinction of a large mink with beautiful, reddish-brown fur. This was the sea mink.

Sea minks lived among the rocks along the American coastline eating mainly fish and shellfish. Because their pelt, or fur coat, was so large and valuable, people hunted them until none were left. The last sea mink was seen in the late 1800's.

Sea minks reportedly were almost 3 feet (1 meter) long, including the tail. That is larger than the American mink, a closely related mustelid that lives today. American minks are also prized for their fur. Many are raised in captivity on mink ranches in various parts of the world.

American mink

How Do Mustelids Help People?

Most members of the weasel family are helpful to people because these animals kill and eat harmful rodents, such as mice and rats. Some members of the weasel family are very active. This means that they need a lot of food, so they kill a lot of rodents.

In some parts of the world, tame mustelids are put to work. For example, fishermen in Southeast Asia have trained small-clawed otters to catch fish for them. People have raised ferrets since the 300's B.C. to control rodents. Scientists believe that tame ferrets are descendants of a wild mustelid known as the European polecat. Today, ferrets are common household pets. They are friendly, playful, and can be taught to use a litter box, like cats.

There are, however, some states in which it is illegal to keep a pet ferret. In these areas, lawmakers fear that pet ferrets will bite or attack humans, although owners of pet ferrets deny that this is likely. And, in some regions the fear is that pet ferrets will escape from captivity, form colonies, and threaten native wildlife.

Domestic ferret

Why Do Some People Dislike Mustelids?

Some people dislike mustelids because they sometimes kill animals that are useful to people. For example, weasels break into chicken coops and kill chickens. Weasels sometimes kill more chickens than they can eat.

Wolverines are known to raid people's reindeer herds in Scandinavia. Fur trappers also believe wolverines kill valuable fur-bearing animals. As a result, many wolverines have been killed as pests. Sometimes, people kill otters because they believe they eat too many shellfish. Some workers at fish farms kill otters to keep them from stealing fish.

Badgers' burrows sometimes cause problems for ranchers. Horses and cattle can injure their legs by stepping in a badger's burrow. And, of course, no one wants to be sprayed by a skunk.

European otter
with fish

 59

Are Mustelids in Danger?

Several members of the weasel family are endangered. Sea otters, giant otters, and several other species of otter are endangered. For hundreds of years, people have hunted otters for their thick, beautiful fur. Water pollution affects all otters, and oil spills have killed sea otters. River otters have also suffered because people have built towns and cities along the rivers where the otters live.

The black-footed ferret is one of the world's most endangered animals. In 1987, only 18 known black-footed ferrets were left. The United States government captured them and began a breeding program to save them from extinction. Since then, the government has reintroduced the animals in several states. South Dakota now has at least 200 black-footed ferrets, but the species in the wild is far from recovered.

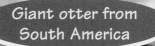

Giant otter from South America

Mustelid Fun Facts

→ Scientists observed one female badger in Minnesota that had 50 burrows in her territory. In summer, she never slept in the same burrow two days in a row.

→ River otters can run at speeds of up to 18 miles (29 kilometers) per hour.

→ Sea otters have the thickest fur of all animals. They have about 650,000 hairs per square inch (6.45 square centimeters). The human scalp may have only about 100,000 hairs.

→ The markings on the faces of skunks and badgers are not there to make them look cute. They probably serve as a warning to other animals that they may get squirted by smelly musk if they do not stay away.

→ Female sea otters sometimes adopt orphaned pups and raise them as their own.

→ Other types of animals, such as rabbits and foxes, make their homes in badger setts (or in parts of setts that are not at that time being used by badgers).

Glossary

boar A male badger.

burrow A hole dug in the ground by an animal for refuge or shelter.

carnivore An animal that eats meat.

carrion The flesh of dead animals that is eaten by other animals.

chamber A place in a sett or burrow where animals sleep, give birth, and raise young.

clan A group of Old World badgers living together.

colony A large group of burrows belonging to prairie dogs, also called a prairie dog town.

extinct A species whose members have died out.

gland An organ in an animal's body that makes a special substance, such as musk.

musk A strong-smelling liquid produced by mustelids to drive away attackers and mark territory.

mustelid An animal belonging to the scientific family Mustelidae, which includes badgers, ferrets, otters, skunks, and weasels.

nutrient A substance in food that helps a living thing grow and live.

omnivore An animal that eats both animals and plants.

pelt The skin of a fur-bearing animal that is used to make clothing.

prey An animal that is caught for food by another animal.

quills Sharp spines on porcupines that can cause painful wounds.

rodent A type of animal whose front teeth never stop growing—including beavers, mice, porcupines, and rats.

sett A vast system of burrows that is dug by Old World badgers.

sow A female badger.

territory An area in which an animal lives and which it defends from many other animals.

Index

(**Boldface** indicates a photo, map, or illustration.)

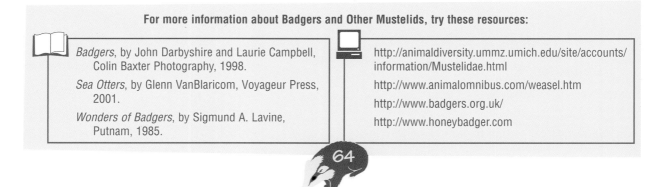

For more information about Badgers and Other Mustelids, try these resources:

Badgers, by John Darbyshire and Laurie Campbell, Colin Baxter Photography, 1998.

Sea Otters, by Glenn VanBlaricom, Voyageur Press, 2001.

Wonders of Badgers, by Sigmund A. Lavine, Putnam, 1985.

http://animaldiversity.ummz.umich.edu/site/accounts/information/Mustelidae.html

http://www.animalomnibus.com/weasel.htm

http://www.badgers.org.uk/

http://www.honeybadger.com

Badger Classification

Scientists classify animals by placing them into groups. The animal kingdom is a group that contains all the world's animals. Phylum, class, order, and family are smaller groups. Each phylum contains many classes. A class contains orders, an order contains families, and a family contains individual species. Each species also has its own scientific name. (The abbreviation "spp." after a genus name indicates that a group of species from a genus is being discussed.) Here is how the animals in this book fit into this system.

Animals with backbones and their relatives (Phylum Chordata)
Mammals (Class Mammalia)
Carnivores (Order Carnivora)

Badgers and Their Relatives (Family Mustelidae)

Badgers (Subfamily Taxidiinae)
American badger . . . . *Taxidea taxus*

Honey badger (Subfamily Mellivorinae)
Ratel, or honey badger . . . . *Mellivora capensis*

Old World badgers (Subfamily Melinae)
Ferret badgers . . . . *Melogale* spp.
Hog badger . . . . *Arctonyx collaris*
Old World, or Eurasian, badger . . . . *Meles meles*
Stink badgers . . . . *Mydaus* spp.

Otters (Subfamily Lutrinae)
American river otters . . . . *Lontra* spp.
Asian small-clawed otter . . . . *Amblonyx cinereus*
Giant otter . . . . *Pteronura brasiliensis*
Old World, or European, river otter . . . . *Lutra lutra*
Sea otter . . . . *Enhydra lutris*

Skunks (Subfamily Mephitinae)
Spotted skunk . . . . *Spilogale* spp.
Striped skunk . . . . *Mephitis mephitis*

Wolverines, martens, weasels, minks (Subfamily Mustelinae)
American mink . . . . *Mustela vison*
Black-footed ferret . . . . *Mustela nigripes*
Ermine, or short-tailed weasel . . . . *Mustela erminea*
European polecat . . . . *Mustela putorius*
Domestic ferret . . . . *Mustela putorius furo*
Least weasel . . . . *Mustela nivalis*
Long-tailed weasel . . . . *Mustela frenata*
Sea mink . . . . *Mustela macrodon*
American pine marten . . . . *Martes americana*
European pine marten . . . . *Martes martes*
Fisher . . . . *Martes pennanti*
Sable . . . . *Martes zibellina*
Wolverine . . . . *Gulo gulo*